A Charlevoix story for Andi!
Love,
Grandma + Grandpa Anderson

This book is dedicated to Diane "Chick" and Bill Picotte, as well as to Trish Morgan, who makes my books so lovely.

Where's Our Siamese? A True Story

Story © 2014 by Suzanne M. Malpass, straddlebooks@gmail.com
Illustrations © 2014 by Trish Morgan, trish@peachbloomhill.com

All rights reserved. No part of this publication may be reproduced or transmitted in any form or by any means, electronic or mechanical, including photocopy, recording, or any information storage and retrieval system, without permission in writing from the publisher.

Requests for permission to excerpt or make copies of any part of the work should be submitted online at info@mascotbooks.com or mailed to Mascot Books, 560 Herndon Parkway #120, Herndon, VA 20170.

PRT0414A

Library of Congress Control Number: 2014935775

Printed in the United States

ISBN-13: 9781620866924

www.mascotbooks.com

Where's Our Siamese?

A True Story

Suzanne M. Malpass

Happy Trails,
Suzanne M. Malpass

Illustrated by
Trish Morgan

Chick was gardening when she heard the commotion. Her husband Bill was washing the car behind their Charlevoix home.

They raced around to the front of the house to check it out. There they found the newspaper delivery man, a confused-looking German Shepherd, an empty cat harness and a large clump of cat fur.

After much effort, the delivery man managed to grab his dog by the collar. Puffing hard, he said, "When my dog saw your big dog statue, she jumped out of the car and attacked. After she found out it wasn't real, she spied your cat and lunged for it."

"Did you see where the cat went?" Chick asked anxiously.

"Yup. While you were comin' around the south side of the house, the cat was escapin' around the north side." He shook his head slowly, "I sure am sorry."

As the man drove away, the couple began calling their pet. They yelled and yelled, but no cat appeared.

When Chick was in tenth grade, her brother gave her a tiny kitten for Christmas. At the time, John and his wife were living in married housing at Michigan State University. Their tiny apartment hardly had room for them and their cat. It certainly had no room for a batch of kittens.

Chick named the Chocolate Point Siamese after the hero of her favorite childhood book. In it, Miss Buttonweezer had named her cat Nimrodent, Hunter of Mice. The cat had been Chick's beloved companion ever since that Christmas ten years ago.

Nim lived up to his name. He caught mice and ate everything but their tails. However, he drew the line at munching on moles. Those he would kill, but never eat.

After Chick married Bill, he became just as attached to the cat. Bill didn't have too much trouble with Nim, even though he developed an allergy to cats.

When there was no response to their calling, Chick and Bill began searching their block. Terrified cats are known to hide in any spot that feels safe. They do not call out to let anyone know where they are.

One place Nim used to hide was under the front porch. He would get so far back, no one could reach him. In the end, Bill put latticework below the porch to keep the cat out.

Even though Nim had taken off toward Michigan Beach, the couple knew he wouldn't go there. Cats hate water! As they walked around, Chick and Bill asked everyone if they'd seen a small, cross-eyed Siamese with a crook in his tail. Some neighbors even joined them in the hunt. The search party looked on porches, peeked under cars, checked behind planters and peered into garages with open doors.

When it got too dark to look, Chick and Bill sat in their living room and stared straight ahead. Neither could think of anything but their missing pet.
"Bill, did I ever tell you about the time I thought Nim was sick? It just was after we got off the ferry on Beaver Island."

"I don't think so."

"When it happened, I went to see that guy on the island who's supposed to know everything about animals."

"I know who you mean."

"The so-called expert said, 'Look how white his gums are. That's a sign of feline leukemia.' So I panicked and caught the ferry back to Charlevoix."

"You did?"

"Uh-huh. When I got to the vet's, he said, 'Oh, for heaven's sake. He was probably just stressed and a bit boat sick. Siamese have lighter gums than other cats anyway.'"

"So, what did you do then?"

"I took the Emerald Isle back to Beaver as soon as I could. But instead of going up on deck, I stayed in the car with Nim on my lap for the whole two hours."

That evening whenever Bill walked past the staircase in the couple's lonely house, he would picture the cat staked out near the top whenever there was company. Nim liked to climb high up and watch everything, but he never joined in the fun.

The next afternoon, Chick took time out from the search to throw in a load of laundry. She smiled as she remembered the time the doorbell rang just after she had opened the dryer. She took off to answer the door.

When she came back, she shut the door to fluff the warm clothes once more. The dryer made a strange thump... thump... thump. *What the heck?* thought Chick. As she opened the door to look inside, a dizzy cat jumped out and made a wobbly exit from the laundry room!

Sometimes when Chick and Bill thought of their little, blue-eyed friend, they smiled through their tears. "Remember the time we took Nim to the park above the beach?" Bill asked as a memory hit him.

Chick nodded, "Nim must have forgotten that he was just a puny, ten-pound cat. He raced down that cliff as if to attack the five big dogs playing in the sand."

"Lucky for Nim they never even noticed him," Bill chuckled. "Once he saw them up close, he couldn't run back to us fast enough."

On one occasion, Chick found a bit of comfort in talking about her missing companion with her dog-crazy neighbors. Ever the schoolteacher, she explained to Cathy and Larry, "Cats are quiet watchers. They are independent and not particularly friendly. Unlike dogs, they don't crave constant human attention. Siamese are even more stand-offish than other cats."

"Boy, that's not like living with Penny!" said Cathy, as she rubbed her big Golden Retriever behind the ears.

"Well, Nim is somewhat different. He's an indoor cat and a lap-sitter," Chick continued wistfully. "As a kitten, he slept wound around my neck. Even after ten years, he still makes his bed wherever I sleep."

For two sad, sad days Chick and Bill called and searched, but there was no sign of their treasured pet. Finally they felt so discouraged, they gave up.

The next day while gardening in the front yard, Chick heard some high, piercing cries. "Bill, come quickly!" she yelled.

"What's up?" asked Bill as soon as he reached her.

"Do you hear that?" They stood still and listened. Then they followed the sound into their back yard. They could hear, but not yet see, a screaming cat. Looking way up into the tall cedar tree, they discovered it was not just any cat. It was Nim!

   Now that they knew he was safe, Chick and Bill wondered how to get the cat down. As a first logical step, Bill got the big extension ladder out of the garage. He leaned it as close as he could to the branch where Nim was clinging.

   Cats are famous for climbing trees in terror and then being too frightened to come back down. Nim was no different. Very slowly, Bill fought his way through the branches until he was near the top of the ladder. All the while, he talked quietly to Nim to keep him calm.

As soon as he could, Bill grabbed the fur of Nim's neck, right where mother cats clamp their teeth to carry their babies. As the cat struggled, Bill's glasses got knocked off and he almost followed them to the ground. "Ouch, Nim!"

"Bill, you be careful way up there!" Chick warned.

"I'm fine, Dear. But his claws are dug so deeply into that bark they won't come loose," he reported to his wife below.

The would-be rescuer stepped up one more rung on the ladder. He grabbed the cat again and pulled as hard as he could, nearly losing his balance. Nim popped free! Bill climbed very slowly down the ladder, with the cat clutched to his chest.

So what did Nim do once he was free? Did he just sit there looking dazed? Did he jump into Chick's waiting arms? Did he run to look for his food and water?

No, no and no. He raced to his litter box!

Afterwards, Bill checked the Siamese all over. He found no injuries other than the loss of fur.

To this day, Chick and Bill believe that Nim cried out so desperately because he needed that litter box! Whatever the reason, they were thrilled to have their family back together and Nim returned to his normal life.

The End

About the author: Suzanne M. Malpass writes under her maiden name in hopes that her many relatives will buy the books when they see their surname on them. Her lifelong love of animals, children and words led to her series of non-fiction children's books, which feature animal rescues with happy endings. *Where's Our Siamese?* is the fifth book in the series.

Suzanne and her rescue dog, Bonita.
Photo by Tina Malpass

Other books by Suzanne M. Malpass:
Stony's Tale: A True Tombstone Story
Rusty Tries Growing Up: A True Eastern Shore Story
A Lab's Tale
Colorado the Flying Horse: A True Arizona Story